real U ®

GUIDE TO

TRAVELING ON YOUR OWN

PETER GREENBERG

Real U Guides

Publisher and CEO:
Steve Schultz

Editor-in-Chief:
Megan Stine

Art Director:
C.C. Krohne

Designer:
David Jackson

Illustration:
Mike Strong

Production Manager:
Alice Todd

Associate Editor:
Cody O. Stine

Copy Editor:
Leslie Fears

Library of Congress Control Number: 2004094757

ISBN: 0-9744159-0-1

First Edition
10 9 8 7 6 5 4 3 2 1

Published by
Real U, Inc.
2582 Centerville Rosebud Rd.
Loganville, GA 30052

www.realuguides.com

Photo Credits:
Cover and Page 1: Martin Sanmiguel/Getty; Page 3: Daniel Allan/Getty; Page 4: Digital Vision/Getty; Page 5: Airline tickets, Don Farrall/Getty; Passport and tickets, ArtToday; Two women in pottery shop, Willie Maldonado/Getty; Leaning tower, ArtToday; Page 6: ArtToday; Page 7: Nick Dolding/Getty; Page 8: Richard Drury/Getty; Page 9:ArtToday; Page 10: Digital Vision/Getty; Page 11: ArtToday; Page 12: Don Farrall/Getty; Page 13: Computer flight search, Don Farrall/Getty; Two woman at computer, ArtToday; Page 14: Legs and baggage, Jack Hollingsworth/Getty; Airline gate, Digital Vision/Getty; Page 16: ArtToday; Page 17: Jim Arbogast/Getty; Page 18: Digital Vision/Getty; Page 19: Golden Gate Bridge, ArtToday; Statue of Liberty, ArtToday; Page 20: Bullet train, ArtToday; Bus, Photodisc Collection/Getty; Page 21: Brown bag lunch, C Squared Studios/Getty; Young man on train platform, J. Clarke/Getty; Page 22: Manchan/Getty; Page 23: Ryan McVay/Getty; Page 24: Steve Schultz; Page 25: Woman stranded with SUV, ArtToday; Map background, ArtToday; Page 26: Plush studios/Getty; Page 27: Ewasko/Getty; Page 28: Patrick Molnar/Getty; Page 29: Frank Herholdt/Getty; Page 30: Christoph Wihelm/Getty; Page 31: Two guys with backpacks, Pando Hall/Getty; Unmade bed, ArtToday; Page 32: Gen Nishino/Getty; Page 33: Mark Downey/Getty; Page 34: Ryan McVay/Getty; Page 35: Taxi bumper, Ryan McVay/Getty; Street scene, ArtToday; Page 36: Train station at night, ArtToday; Bus interior, ArtToday; Page 37: Mini Cooper, Megan Stine; Parking sign, Thinkstock/Getty; Page 38: Kareem Black/Getty; Page 39: ArtToday; Page 40: Photodisc Collection/Getty; Page 41: Baggage claim, ArtToday; Passport office, Ghislain & Marie David de Lossy/Getty; Page 42: ArtToday; Page 43: ArtToday; Page 44: ArtToday; Page 45: Martin Sanmiguel/Getty; Page 46: Map background, ArtToday; Man looking at passport, Burke/Triolo Productions/Getty; Page 47: ArtToday; Page 48: Jorg Greuel/Getty; Page 50: Ryan McVay/Getty; Page 51: ArtToday; Page 53: ArtToday; Page 54: ArtToday; Page 55: ArtToday; Page 56: British phone booth, ArtToday; Man on cell phone, Kaz Chiba/Getty; Page 57: ArtToday; Page 58: Larry Dale Gordon/Getty; Page 59: Cheyenne Rouse/Getty; Page 60: Willie Maldonado/Getty; Page 61: Richard Drury/Getty; Page 62: Andersen Ross/Getty; Back cover: Travel Channel.

realU

GUIDE TO

TRAVELING ON
YOUR OWN

PETER GREENBERG

So you're ready to hit the road...

There's good news and there's bad news about traveling on your own: The good news is that you're actually on your own—as in off the couch, out of the house, and out in the real world—all of which can be a lot of fun if you know how to navigate airports, purchase last minute train tickets, and just basically get from here to wherever.

Of course, the bad news is also that you're on your own—off that comfy couch, out of your parents' lovely house, and very much out in the real world—which can be anything from mildly inconvenient to abjectly terrifying.

O.K., so maybe you fall into that second category—a few luggage labels short of world-class-traveler status. Maybe navigating a foreign train station sounds about as easy as performing your own appendectomy, and you still pack three suitcases for a three-day weekend at the beach.

But don't worry. We've got all the answers for you, whether you're headed for Spring Break, a week visiting colleges in the Northeast, or even a summer gallivanting across as much of Europe as you can cover before the cash runs out.

So turn the page and find out everything you need to know in order to get there cheaply, safely, and in one piece.

And welcome to 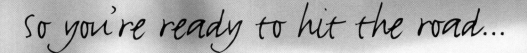 realU®

GUIDE TO TRAVELING ON YOUR OWN
TABLE OF CONTENTS

ARE YOU A SAVVY TRAVELER?

There are basically two types of travelers in the world: Those who think that losing their passport somewhere outside a remote Siberian village in the middle of the night is simply "part of the fun," and those who see the words "Youth Hostel" on a sign and assume that the local teenagers are irrationally unfriendly and should be avoided at all costs.

So which one are you? Have you got what it takes to survive travel trauma of various types—or do you still consider "no room service" to be the scariest phrase in the English language? Take this quiz and find out!

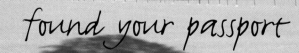

found your passport

1.

Let's say you're traveling with your best friend on a backpacking trip through Europe, and, as best friends, you're making all the decisions together—where to go, what to do, where to stay, etc. Everything's great until the very last week of your trip, when your best friend insists that she "simply must see Rome before she dies," while you want nothing more than to spend your last few days with the hunky Barcelonan Beefcake you picked up in a discothèque last night. Neither one of you wants to budge. Your solution?

A. Sneak out in the middle of the night, taking nothing but the jeans you're wearing and your best friend's hair dryer. Call your parents collect and beg them to fly you and the Barcelonan Beefcake back to Pittsburgh.

B. Sneak out in the middle of the night, taking all of your belongings—plus all the shared belongings, like the toiletries, the canned soups, extra cash, maps and guide books, and your ex-best friend's favorite denim skirt which you've been wanting to borrow for a month. And the phone card.

C. Compromise: Take the Spaniard with you to Rome. Or spend a few days here, a few days there. Or go to Rome and write scintillating postcards back to Barcelona. Anything to keep the peace and keep the trip from falling apart.

Ooh Ricardo

2.

You're visiting a friend in Chicago, and it's up to you to book the flight. This shouldn't pose much of a problem for you, since you've always known that flights tend to be cheaper if you book them...

A. A few days before you want to fly.
B. In your most sultry telephone voice.
C. Two weeks or more before you want to fly.

3.

Assuming for the moment that you make it to Chicago with a little money still to your name, what's your plan once you get to the airport?

A. Hop into the first cab you see—or better yet, go up to one of those limo drivers at the airport, claim that you're Mr. Smith from Chemicore, and see where you end up. Nothing like a free ride, right?
B. Well, your sultry telephone voice hasn't failed you yet...call your friend and beg to get picked up.

C. Follow the airport signs for "Ground Transportation," then see if you can find a cheap shuttle bus or rail line into the city. After all, you know your sultry telephone voice comes off as husky and possibly laryngitis-infected in person.

4.

So what do you do if you lose your passport in a remote Siberian village in the middle of the night?

A. Cry.
B. Phone home. Then cry.
C. Contact the American Embassy or U.S. Consulate immediately and tell them your problem. Use the back-up forms of ID you brought with you in order to get a new passport.

5.

A visa is:

A. Something which foreign citizens have to deal with when they want to come to America—i.e., not your problem.
B. Your favorite credit card.
C. An entry permit issued by a foreign government, which you'll need in order to get into certain countries.

SCORING:

If you survived the jokes in this quiz, you're already in good shape for traveling on your own or with your friends. After all, there's no way the beds in a youth hostel could be as un-funny as this is. That said, some people are better equipped for travel than others—so tote up your score and see where you fall. A and B answers aren't worth diddly. Give yourself one point for each C answer.

0-1 Points:
Ouch. We're glad you're eager to get on the road, but are you sure you're ready to navigate the countryside alone? Read on, and we'll make it as painless as possible.

2-3 Points:
Crying until someone takes pity on you clearly isn't your first choice when faced with a problem, and that's good. Unfortunately, it seems to be your second choice, and that could probably use a little work. Dry your eyes, check out the tips in this book, and no one will ever have to take pity on you again.

4-5 Points:
Good for you—you're well on your way to becoming a savvy traveler. Read on to learn even more tips for how to manage when you're out on your own.

don't lose them!

GETTING

THERE

Unless you decide to walk—which we don't recommend, especially if you're planning on traveling to Europe—there are four main ways to get from here to there. (O.K., five if you include ships and six if you insist on including hot air balloons—but don't be difficult.)

Flying (in planes) has become the most common way to travel, and it's usually the cheapest way, too. But there are times when it makes more sense to take a train, car, or bus. For example, if you're moving into a dorm 200 miles from home, you'll want to drive. (It can be rough loading your futon into the overhead compartment on a plane.) And how about short jaunts? You'd probably spend more time just going through security at the airport than it takes to go from New York to Philadelphia by train.

In short, planes, trains, buses, and cars each have their own advantages and drawbacks. Here's the lowdown on how to get the most out of each form of travel.

Only 1,543 miles to Paris!

FLIGHT SCHOOL

Of all the ways to travel, air travel probably has the widest range of ticket prices—from super-low standby tickets for around $50, to round-trip tickets booked in desperation the night before, which could easily run you more than a thousand dollars. The goal, then, is to avoid the latter and hunt for the former. Here are some tips.

BUY EARLY

If you decide to fly, the first thing you should do is go online a few months in advance and research airlines and prices. Tickets are almost always cheaper two weeks to 45 days in advance. That's especially true for peak travel times like summer, Thanksgiving, or the winter holidays.

BUY LATE

One exception to the rule that flights are cheaper if you buy early is the fact that many airlines offer last-minute discounts. These last minute discounts come in a couple of different forms. Some airlines offer standby discounts—you show up at the airport, say you want to fly standby, and hope to get on a flight. Generally, you can't check any baggage with this kind of trip, but the discounts can be really deep. See Page 15 for details on one particularly cheap standby program called X-Fares. Other last minute discounts some airlines offer are web specials. You can either sign up to be on an airline's e-mail list, or simply check the airline's web site for discounted specials, usually offered about a week before you want to fly.

Flight Search

Quick Flight Search

Number of passengers

Service

One way   Round trip

From

BUNDLE OF SAVINGS

Look for "bundled" deals on the Internet. These are offers that include not just air-fare, but hotels and even rental cars. In a growing number of cases, you'll discover that the bundled deal can be cheaper than buying the airfare by itself! Oddly, this can end up being the best deal, even if you don't need the hotel.

BUY OFTEN

Even if you don't think of yourself as a frequent flyer, there's no reason not to sign up for frequent flyer programs with the airlines that you do fly. It's free to join these programs and the miles you accumulate will eventually add up to free tickets, upgrades, magazine subscriptions, your own jet (you wish), and more.

LOYAL AND TRUE

You'll always have to shop around in order to find the best fares, but the more you can stick to one airline, the faster your frequent flyer miles will add up. That means you're saving money in the long run because eventually you get to fly for free.

BUY ONLINE

Many airlines offer discounted fares that are only available on their web sites. Others may offer the same fare online that you'd get if you called, but they give you extra frequent flyer miles if you buy online. Who knew the Internet was useful for something other than ripping off the music industry?

more flight school →

VOLUNTEER TO BE DUMPED

Or rather bumped, as they say in the airline industry. What's the deal? Well, airlines often overbook and sell too many tickets for a flight. When that happens, they'll need to bump someone off the flight. If your plans are flexible, you can turn it to your advantage by volunteering to be "bumped," which means you take a later flight in exchange for bonuses from the airline. Typically these bonuses come in the form of flight vouchers, free hotel stays, meals, or discounted tickets. Some smart travelers march up to the desk at the gate and automatically volunteer to be bumped every time they fly. Free tickets —whee!

PLAN AHEAD

Canceling or changing flight plans can cost you $100 to $150—so don't book a flight until you're sure about when you want to fly. If you must cancel your trip, hang on to your "non-refundable" ticket. In many cases, you'll be able to use it later (within one year) by simply paying a change fee and any increase in the fare.

bump me—please!

There actually is a best day of the week to buy airline tickets— Wednesday.

TRAVEL LIGHT

Some airlines charge an excess baggage fee of 1 percent of a full first-class fare for every kilogram over the accepted weight— even if you only booked a coach flight! Other airlines charge a flat fee, usually from $100 to $125. And oversized items like bicycles or llama cages will also add a tidy amount to your ticket price—sometimes as much as $150 for that bicycle. (Don't even ask about the llama!)

ONLY ON WEDNESDAYS

Under the "strange but true" category, there actually is a best day of the week to buy airline tickets—Wednesday. And there's even a best time on Wednesday to buy—around midnight. Why Wednesday? Because that's when the fare wars between airlines start each week. Small airlines offer lower prices on Wednesday, usually around midnight, to both entice would-be travelers and prompt big companies to drop their prices. The bigger airlines usually follow suit—for a few days, anyway. Come Friday, most prices have gone up, but for that two-day window, you might get your hands on a pretty good deal.

Rocking the Student Discount

O.K., we know that the photo on your student I.D. makes you look like you've just finished giving a couple of pints of blood at the Red Cross, more or less involuntarily. But that ridiculous portrait may also be your key to some pretty decent travel savings. If you're a student, you qualify for various services which help you get discounts on travel.

Airtran, for example, offers a program called X-Fares that lets students fly stand-by for about $55 bucks during the school year. Basically you just show up at the ticket counter and pay $55 for a one-way flight. (Long-haul flights are $75 one way.) You can't fly on Fridays or Sundays, you can't check your luggage, and you're limited to one carry-on bag. You'll need proof of age since the X-Fares are only available for 18-to-22-year-olds.

Students get a break on train and bus travel, too. Just sign up for either the Student Advantage card or the International Student Exchange I.D. Both get you 15% discounts on all Amtrak train and Greyhound bus travel. And although you have to pay a fee to sign up for these cards, if you're planning on taking the train between college and your home town, or visiting friends fairly frequently, it may pay off in the long run. These cards also offer discounts on hotel stays and other travel-related expenses. Go to www.studentadvantage.com and www.isecard.com for more information.

4 CLEARED FOR TAKEOFF: MORE TIPS FOR PLANE TRAVEL

1 CHECK FLIGHT STATUS ONLINE

It's nearly impossible to avoid all airport delays. There's a big difference between whether a flight is scheduled to leave on time and whether the plane is actually en route. Hey, the Titanic was scheduled to be on time and we all know what happened there. Even in the astronomically unlikely event that you never have to wait for a late flight, it will take you half an hour to get a chai latté at the airport coffee shop. However, there's one easy way to avoid waiting at the airport for hours while your plane circles O'Hare. Almost every airline lets you check the status of flights online. They'll actually tell you if your flight is expected to be late. Check the web site before you leave home, and if your flight is late, maybe you've got time to catch *As the World Turns* after all. (You can also call the airline if you don't feel like going online—however, you may have to navigate a dozen telephone menus and wait on hold before you get any information.)

Check the airline's web site before you leave home to find out if your flight is delayed.

2 CHECK IN ONLINE

Many airlines now let you check in and print boarding passes online, usually up to 24 hours before your flight. If you've ever seen the lines at the ticketing counter on Memorial Day weekend, you know why printing your ticket out at home can be immensely helpful. Some airlines even let you pick your own seat assignment. Can anyone say "Exit Row?" (Hint: Exit rows have more leg room. Go for it whenever you can!)

3 BRING YOUR FLIGHT INFORMATION

Even if you can't check in online, print out the page with your confirmation number and flight info and bring it to the airport. At the very least, your confirmation number may help you expedite the check-in process. Some airports have check-in kiosks where you can scan your electronic ticket's barcode (or enter a frequent flyer number, or slide your credit card) to get your boarding pass. And if there's any conflict about your reservation, the hard copy of your e-ticket reservation may help you resolve the tiff.

4 ACING THE AIRPORT

Getting to the airport—and navigating the airport once you're there—can be an ordeal in and of itself. Here are some tips:

- Airport parking tends to be pricey. Your best bet is to ask a friend to drop you off—and pick you up, too.

- If you have to park at the airport, there will usually be a number of choices. Hourly parking is usually right next to the airport, but it's often exorbitantly priced if you're going out of town for more than, well, an hour. Economy parking will be farther from the airport, but there will usually be a free shuttle, and your budget will thank you when you get back.

- Every airport is different, but they're all made up of the same basic parts, which should be marked in easy-to-read signs. Turn the page for a quick look at where to go and what to do when you get there.

AIRPORT SIGNS

CURBSIDE CHECK-IN:
There might not be a sign, but at larger airports you'll see the curbside check-in stands in front of the terminal. This is often the fastest and easiest place to check your bags and get a boarding pass.

TICKETING AND CHECK-IN:
Go here if there's no curbside check-in. You'll also have to go to the ticket counter if you need to make a change to your routing, or if you don't already have a seat assignment and boarding pass.

TERMINAL AND GATES:
This is where you get on the plane. What, you thought you could hail it from the curb, like a taxi? Larger airports have several different terminals, usually lettered A, B, C, and so forth. The gates within each terminal are usually numbered. Be sure to arrive at the gate at least 30 minutes before your flight departs. Boarding usually starts 20-30 minutes ahead of time.

BAGGAGE CLAIM:
Picking up your bags is what goes on in this section of the airport. Look for signs with your flight number to find out which carousel your bags will be on. Or just follow the crowd from your plane.

MEN:
Usually there's a restroom behind that door. Think twice about opening it if you're a woman.

WHICH IS
CHEAPER?

Check out this chart for cost comparisons. Our example shows what it typically costs to travel from San Francisco to New York City, round trip.

PLANE

$203 round trip from San Francisco to New York (JFK). Add $23 for ground transportation into New York City and back to the airport.

BUS

$236 round trip from San Francisco to New York, with seven-day advance purchase. This fare assumes you have a 15% student discount card.

TRAIN

$255 round trip for an Amtrak ticket, with a student discount card. Meals not included.

CAR

$1,010 round trip which includes gas, tolls, meals, and 4 nights each way in a cheap motel on the road. If a friend shares the driving, add another $200 for meals for 10 days. Cost per person: $605.

HITTING THE
RAILS & ROADS

Although plane travel is often the cheapest, it may make more sense to take a train or bus for short distances between cities—especially in Europe, where the rail system is extensive and often cheaper.

What's more, the scenery is much more, well, scenic, when you're not 30,000 feet above it. (And take our word—the absence of a "Fasten Seatbelt" sign is a definite plus when it comes to making friends with your neighbors.)

Booking train and bus travel is generally much simpler than booking flights, since there are only two main carriers—Amtrak for trains, and Greyhound for bus service. You can get a lot of the information you need from their web sites: www.amtrak.com and www.greyhound.com. But here are a few tips to remember.

■ Ticket prices for most trains in the U.S. will not be cheaper if you book them early, but that's no reason to postpone making a reservation. Trains can fill up (especially around peak travel times like holidays), and reserving in advance allows you to bypass long lines at the ticket counter.

■ Ticket prices on Greyhound buses are cheaper if you book seven days or more in advance. However, advance-fare tickets are non-refundable, whereas tickets bought at the bus terminal are generally refundable if you change your mind at the last minute about whether it's really a good idea to visit that girl you met on the Internet at her parents' house in Cleveland.

Although many trains have a snack car, with your luck it won't be open when you're hungry. Think: bag lunch.

■ Little discounts can make a big difference. Some examples:

- Student Advantage Card members get 15% off Amtrak and Greyhound tickets.
- If you're a AAA member, you can save on Amtrak tickets.
- Greyhound gives you 10% off just for booking online.

■ Travel light. On some trains, there's no such thing as "checked baggage." In other words, whatever you bring, you carry—and you hoist up onto the luggage rack. This is especially true in Europe. (Good luck with that steamer trunk.) On the other hand, many Amtrak trains allow you to check baggage, so call ahead and find out.

■ Although many trains have a snack car or dining car, with your luck it won't be open when you're hungry, and will be pretty expensive when it finally is open (and by then you're not hungry). Think: bag lunch.

■ Most buses and some trains make a fair number of stops between major cities, increasing the length of the trip. You can check schedules online. Often, driving would be faster.

■ On the other hand, taking the train when you've got to get from Cleveland to Philly in a blizzard in the middle of the night may be a better choice—especially if for some strange reason your parents won't lend you the Benz.

See Page 54 for special tips on traveling by train in other countries.

semester break...

CLICK AND GO: BOOKING TRAVEL ONLINE

You already know that booking flights or trains online has benefits, like discounted fares and no hold music. But are there drawbacks? Sure—maybe you like hold music.

The Internet is an excellent resource that goes beyond simply booking flights on airline web sites. It can also act as a virtual travel agent, helping you find great deals and bargain packages. Sites like Expedia.com and Travelocity.com both offer automated searches for the cheapest airfares to a given city—which is theoretically what a travel agent would be doing if you hired one. But these sites can also help you find discounted hotel rooms and vacation packages—a real asset for travel novices or people who simply don't have time to hunt for deals themselves.

There are, however, two possible problems with booking travel through an Internet middleman. First, anytime you use a middleman, there's one more piece that can go wrong—one more reservation or confirmation number that can get lost, for example. And although web sites like these base their reputations on getting things right, accidents can still happen.

The second problem is that tickets booked through online travel sites tend to be non-refundable. And although this is true of some discount tickets booked directly through the airline as well, chances are you'll know where the loopholes are if you book everything—and read all the fine print—yourself.

One good solution is to use these web sites as a research tool. Search for the cheapest fares to your destination, find out which airline has the lowest prices, and then go directly to the airline to see if you can get that fare—or a better one! (Since most of these web sites charge a $5 service fee, you ought to be able to save at least 5 bucks.)

For more on using online resources to book hotels, check out Page 28.

TOP 15 WEB SITES FOR YOUNG TRAVELERS

www.expedia.com (travel packages and rates)

www.travelocity.com (travel packages and rates)

www.studentuniverse.com (kind of like Expedia for students, with discount travel booking)

www.hotwire.com (unique travel packages and rates)

www.site59.com (last-minute travel guide)

www.travisa.com (quick passports and visas)

www.travel.state.gov/visa/americans (list of countries that require visas)

www.oanda.com (fast conversion rates for foreign currency)

www.aphis.usda.gov/travel (food you can and can't bring into the United States)

www.hostels.com (information about hostels around the world)

www.hiayh.org (official web site of Hostelling International USA)

www.wordreference.com (dictionary web site)

www.subwaynavigator.com (subway routes around the world)

www.cdc.gov/travel (list of immunization requirements for each country)

www.eurail.com (train travel in Europe)

TRAVEL AGENTS: WHAT ARE THEY GOOD FOR?

Before the Internet travel boom, travel agents were more popular and often more essential then they are today. But now web sites have taken over the functions travel agents once performed—putting together package deals, searching for discounts, booking flights and hotels.

Thanks to the Internet, doing it yourself is quicker, gives you more control over your travel plans, and saves you costly agent fees.

But that doesn't mean travel agents are useless. Travel agents have managed to stay in business primarily by focusing on niche markets like cruise ships, handicapped travel, remote countries, and luxury packages, and they're still as good as ever at booking these things. Also, many agents may know how to save money by taking unusual routes—flying to Chicago, then to Vancouver, for instance, instead of taking a direct flight. And travel agents do all of the work for you, so if you don't have the time or inclination to search for the best deals, a travel agent may be the way to go.

If you decide to go with a travel agent, check with friends and family for recommendations. Hopefully you'll get at least a name or two. Call them up and just start asking questions. If that agent is worth his or her salt, and values good business tactics, he will be as honest and straightforward with you as possible. Good agents, if they are unable to help you, will usually refer you to someone who can.

TRAVEL AGENTS FOCUS ON NICHE MARKETS LIKE CRUISE SHIPS, HANDICAPPED TRAVEL, REMOTE COUNTRIES, AND LUXURY PACKAGES

ON THE ROAD: TRAVELING BY CAR

The lure of the open road is legendary, although when you've been in enough truck stop restrooms, you'll begin to wonder why. That said, road trips have huge pros, and a few pretty big cons, as well. Here's our run-down:

PROS

- If three or more people are traveling, this may be the cheapest way to go.

- Offers nearly unlimited freedom in choosing the route and stopping points along the way.

- Obviously, traveling by car is the easiest way to transport large items, like furniture.

- Road trip anecdotes, novels, folk songs, etc. are generally much less entertaining if they take place in coach class of a plane.

CONS

- Gas, tolls, food, and lodging add up pretty quickly on a road trip. Flying would often be cheaper, especially if only one or two people are sharing the expense of the trip.

- There's always the matter of where to stay. Although you'll be tempted to sleep in your car, don't do it—it's unsafe in many areas, and illegal in some states.

- Driving long distances gets to be less fun after the first month or so. Hiring a chauffeur with a British accent is prohibitively expensive.

- If you're traveling to a big city, you will probably have to pay to park your car once you get there. This expense can add up faster than you can say, "Isn't it your turn to pay for dinner?"

where am I?

HOME AWAY

FROM HOME: WHERE TO STAY

If you had your way, you'd find the cheapest airfare, bum a free ride to the airport, take a free airport-to-hotel shuttle to your destination, and then check into the most lavish, expensive, luxuriously appointed Presidential suite at the Ritz and kick back in a terrycloth robe, right?

But the reality is that you'll often be stuck inspecting the sheets at the El Thrifty Motor Inn, hoping you don't find anything moving—or worse, inspecting the sheets on your bachelor uncle's pull-out sofa-bed, hoping you don't find anything moving!

Yes, not for everyone, the glamorous jet-setting hotel life. That's why it helps if you have a few tips on how to get your money's worth at hotels, hostels, even your relatives' houses—or at least how to get a set of clean sheets.

best I could find!

LIVING IT UP: HOTELS AND MOTELS

Hotels and motels are never going to be as cheap as your Aunt Estelle's guest room. But if you know how to work the system, you can usually find a room at a pretty decent rate—and you won't have to share a closet with Estelle's muumuus from the 1960's. Here's how to wheel and deal with the hotel industry.

SHOP AROUND

Of course some hotels will be cheaper than others, and it doesn't take much to figure out which ones. (Hint: It's the ones without the mint on your pillow...or without the pillow, in some cases.) But even after you've picked your hotel, there are ways to shop around. You can generally book a hotel either through its web site, through its national toll-free number (if it's part of a big hotel chain), by calling the specific hotel and speaking to someone at the front desk, or by going through a travel agent or travel web site. Different methods will yield better results at different times: If the hotel is empty and desperate, calling the front desk will get you a better rate than calling the national toll-free number. If you're traveling at a peak time, online travel sites like Expedia, Travelocity, or Hotels.com may be able to find you a discount. And sometimes the hotel web sites offer "web only" discounts, just to keep you on your toes. Look alive, sailor!

ASK FOR EVERY DISCOUNT IMAGINABLE

Almost every hotel offers some kind of discount for AAA members. Many offer discounts to Student Advantage card members. Guess what? They won't give you the discount if you don't ask—even if you *are* wearing your embroidered "I'm a AAA Member" polo shirt.

WATCH OUT FOR ADD-ONS

Another important thing to remember when booking a hotel: Most hotels will neglect to mention that the rate offered to you, even if it's the lowest available, doesn't include occupancy tax, or local or state sales taxes. They call these taxes "add-ons," and they can really "add up" if you're not careful—especially in big cities, where taxes are higher. Sometimes your final bill will be 25% higher than you expected! So ask, and then budget accordingly.

RESERVATIONS ABOUT RESERVATIONS

When you're making hotel reservations, the fine print can get a little complicated. Check out these basic rules to keep from getting burned by a guy in a silly jacket and a name tag:

■ Unless you book through a travel agent, your reservation comes in the form of a confirmation number, which you'll need when you get to the front desk. This is how you prove you've really got a reservation.

■ Your confirmation number usually confirms that you'll show up at the hotel before 6:00 p.m. on the day of your arrival, and that you'll pay the amount you agreed upon when you made the reservation. This is key: Without a reservation and confirmation number, the room rate isn't set, and may be different by the time you get from your house in Pittsburgh to the front desk in New Orleans.

■ Generally, you can cancel your reservation until 6:00 p.m. on the day of your arrival. Sometimes, though, especially in big cities, hotels require 24-hour notice for cancellation, which means you've got until 6:00 p.m. the day before you arrive. You should always ask about the hotel's cancellation policy when you reserve your room.

■ Generally, there's no canceling a reservation made with one of the online travel sites.

■ If you know you're getting in after 6:00 p.m., you can guarantee your room for late arrival. This generally means you have to give a credit card number, and if you don't show up at all, they charge your credit card anyway. But it also means they don't give away the room after 6:00 p.m. to someone else. It's yours, no matter how late you arrive.

Unless you book through a travel agent, your reservation comes in the form of a confirmation number, which you will need when you get to the front desk.

YOUTH HOSTELS

Youth hostels are a great way to save a buck and meet travelers who haven't showered in several weeks. But with rates as low as about $15 a night, who cares if your roommates are a bit ripe? Although hostels come in many shapes and sizes, they're all based on the same basic philosophy: cheap beds and not much else. Here are some facts about hostelling to get you started.

■ The classic hostels are "dormitories"— think summer-camp-style rooms with a bunch of bunk beds. Usually men and women sleep in separate dormitories, and share communal bathrooms.

■ All hostels provide a blanket and pillow, but you need to bring your own sheet. Hostels recommend that you get a "sleeping sheet"—basically a sheet sewn together into a sleeping bag shape. Actual sleeping bags generally aren't allowed.

■ You'll also have to bring your own soap and towel.

■ Most hostels recommend but don't require reservations. The room rates don't fluctuate (except during peak times), so you don't have to worry about booking in advance, but popular hostels do tend to fill up.

■ Expect to play by different rules at different hostels. Some have a curfew by which you must be in the hostel or face getting locked out. Others have "lock-out" time during the day— usually between 10:00 a.m. and 5:00 p.m.—when, as they say, you don't have to go home, but you can't stay here. Most hostels ask you to help clean up in the common areas (kitchen, lounge, etc.).

■ Although it may sound like hostels are pretty heavy on the rules and regs, you're still getting a cheap room, often in a great location. Urban hostels tend to be located right in the middle of the city, and a few of the rural hostels are in old lighthouses, castles, factories— Hostelling International's web site even boasts a hostel in a Swedish sailing ship! For comprehensive lists of hostels, and to make reservations, check out www.hiayh.org (the Hostelling International USA web site) or www.hostels.com.

Youth hostels are a great way to save a buck with rates as low as $15 a night!

CRASHING WITH FAMILY AND FRIENDS

If you're lucky, you'll have family or friends where you're headed. And if you're really lucky, they'll still be willing to call you their family and/or friend after you've crashed on their couch for a week.

Obviously, crashing in Aunt Estelle's guest room doesn't require a lot of bargaining or shopping around, but it does require tact and certain social graces. To make sure it goes well, check out our Crash Course in Crashing Etiquette:

■ The first rule of staying with family or friends is that it's best to call weeks— or even months—in advance to let them know you're coming to town and ask if you can stay.

■ Don't expect to be fed. Of course, you know and we know that your Aunt Estelle isn't going to let you go hungry, and will probably insist that you take more tuna noodle casserole than you know what to do with. But it's only polite to assume that you're on your own when it comes to meals. And that doesn't mean raiding the fridge, thank you very much.

■ Make the bed. And keep the bathroom clean and relatively free of your overflowing cornucopia of toiletries and hair care products. The less your hosts notice that you're there, the more willing they'll be to have you back in the future.

■ Try to let your hosts know when you're leaving and when you'll be coming back. Sure, they're not the boss of you, but they are the ones who have to leave a light burning in the kitchen so you don't stub your toe when you come in late.

don't forget to make the bed!

31

AROUND

Getting from home to your destination can be fun. But if you really believe that getting there is half the fun, you're either having more fun than we are in coach class, or you're not having nearly enough fun once you get where you're going.

One key to having a great time in any destination is knowing how to get around in unfamiliar territory. You don't want to spend half of your first day in San Francisco just trying find those famous cable cars, do you? Or worse—standing on the street corner, staring at them, trying to figure out how to grab a ride. (Hint: It's easiest to get on at the beginning of the line, rather than trying to board a moving vehicle on a 45 degree angle hill!) In short, the best plan is to scope out the city buses, subways, trolleys, and airport limos in advance—and check out a map of the city, too. That way you'll be able to take the city by storm and start enjoying your vacation from day one.

So turn the page. We've got some tips for making the bulk of your trip more than 50% fabulous.

wheee!

GROUND TRANSPORTATION:
GETTING OUT OF THE AIRPORT

Almost every major airport will have a row of taxis waiting for you right outside the "Baggage Claim and Ground Transportation" doors. Taxis are definitely the easiest way to get from the airport to your hotel, or hostel, or cardboard box in the park. However, after you've paid the fare from the airport to downtown metropolis— think close to $30 or $40 in New York, for example—you may have no choice but to sleep in that cardboard box in the park.

If you want to avoid the expense of a taxi, visit the web site for the airport you're flying into and click on "Ground Transportation." You should find a list of transportation options— buses, trains, rickshaws, etc. Particularly useful (and free!) are the airport-to-hotel shuttles that are provided by hotels in major cities.

Of course, it's even more useful to have a friend in the city who can tell you what bus to take or what train line to get on. But beware! The one person you don't want to take advice from is the stranger who approaches you outside the airport offering to get you a cab. These guys sound very official, but don't fall for it. They're offering you "gypsy" cabs, which are illegal and can be unsafe. This is a common ploy at most big city airports, but only tourists fall for this trap.

If you think you'll be taking a taxi after all, it can't hurt to call 1-800-TAXICAB before you leave. Ask to be connected to a cab company in the city you're flying to, and then find out whether they offer flat rate fares from the airport (which some cities do), and whether they accept credit cards (which most taxis don't).

After you've paid the fare from the airport, you may have to sleep in a cardboard box.

CITY SPEAK:
HOW TO GET AROUND

The best way to get around a city varies from traveler to traveler. For example, you may be there to see the sights and take in the feel of the city at a leisurely pace, while the hastily-chosen travel companion you met on craigslist.org wants to race from one landmark to the next as if the guidebook were some kind of crazy scavenger hunt, and whoever finishes first wins. For you—the walking tour. For him—taxis. Read on to learn the fine points of each kind of city transportation.

write down that cab number

Be Taxi Smart

Here are some quick tips to help you get the most out of your $20 cab ride.

■ Read all the signs posted inside the cab, facing the backseat. They'll often tell you about your rights.

■ Don't take "gypsy" cabs—it's not safe.

■ Make sure the driver starts the meter, if there is one. You don't want to argue about the price of the ride when you reach your destination.

■ When you get into the cab, write down the cab number, especially if you've got luggage or packages with you inside the cab. You'll find the cab's license number next to the driver's picture—on the dashboard or the glass partition, in most cabs. If you leave something in the cab, you're pretty much out of luck unless you have the cab's number. If you have it, you can call the taxi company or local transit authority, tell them what happened, and find out how to retrieve your lost bags.

■ Tip 10-15%. That way, if you leave your bag in the cab, you might actually get it back.

MASS TRANSIT 101

Navigating unfamiliar mass transit systems takes a bit of practice, especially if you didn't grow up in a city with a mass transit system. But although every city's subway and bus system is different, there are a few similarities which ought to get you started and save you from mass embarrassment. Here are some tips:

- Get a map. They're generally free, and can be picked up at the ticket window of most subway stations.

- Although subway and bus maps will seem pretty inscrutable at first, there is a logic to them. It may help to compare the subway map to a real map.

- Subways usually require either a token (one token will be equal to one fare, generally) or a fare card of some sort (usually a paper card with a magnetic stripe). You'll be able to buy tokens or a fare card at the subway station, either from a ticket window or a machine.

- Mass transit fare cards are good for a dollar amount—whatever you paid for them—and the machine will deduct the fare from your balance until the money's gone. You can usually add value to your fare card, and you can find out how much it's worth by putting it in the card reader machine.

- Buses, like subways, often require a metro card and won't accept cash. If they do take real money, you'll need to have exact change. And when we say change, we mean change—many bus systems won't accept dollar bills, so be prepared with plenty of quarters if you don't have a token or fare card.

- Fares differ widely from city to city, as does the way fares are calculated. In New York, subways and buses charge a flat rate no matter where you're going; in San Francisco and Washington, D.C., the rate changes depending on the distance of your journey; and in Boston, you'll pay twice as much if you're a Yankees fan. That is, if they let you on the bus in one piece.

- Finally, you will identify yourself as an out-of-towner by sticking your fare card in the slot the wrong way. Don't sweat it; happens to the best of us.

RENTING CARS

■ Many rental car agencies (especially Avis and Hertz) make it extremely difficult to rent a car if you're under the age of twenty-five. (This doesn't apply in New York, where Hertz lost an age discrimination court case and now rents to people between eighteen and twenty-four. The court case doesn't keep them from charging a hefty $56-per-day additional fee to young punks, however.)

■ Other companies' policies vary. For example, Alamo, Budget, and especially Dollar will all rent to drivers between the ages of twenty-one and twenty-five, but they'll charge you a higher rate.

■ The car rental company will ask if you want to purchase car renters' insurance. Our advice: Don't do it. Check with your automobile insurance carrier—most policies cover vehicles under your temporary use. Also, if you book your car using a major credit card, the card may provide coverage (but check with them first to be sure).

← don't you wish?

BABY YOU CAN DRIVE MY CAR, BUT GOOD LUCK PARKING IT

If city driving can be a real pain in the, um, blind spot, actually parking your car in a major city can hit you where it really hurts: right in the check book. However, there are some trips for which a car comes in handy—and some trips you really couldn't do without one. If you must drive into a big, unfamiliar city, try to have someone riding shotgun who can read a map and help you navigate.

37

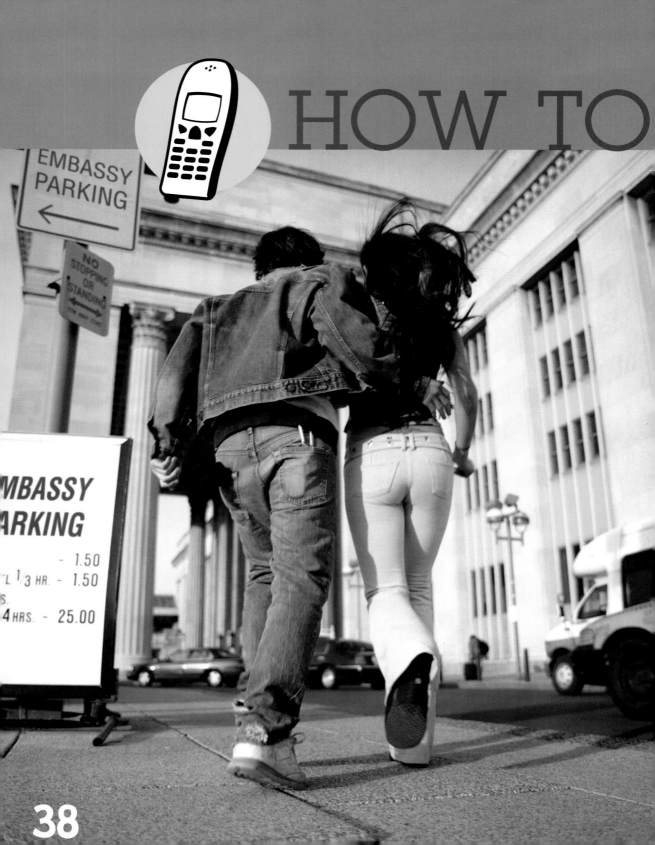

COPE WITH EMERGENCIES

There are various ways to deal with emergencies. You can weep and moan after they happen because you didn't see them coming, or you can weep and moan after they happen because you did see them coming, but failed to prepare yourself.

The fact is that every emergency, no matter how inconvenient, is ultimately manageable, especially if you plan ahead. And while not every emergency is avoidable, problems like lost luggage, lost tickets, lost dignity, even lost passports can all be dealt with, and with a minimum of hysteria, if you've got the proper know-how. Read on for good advice about how to cope and how to prepare.

lost my passport...

GONE!
HOW TO COPE WITH LOSING STUFF

Needless to say, you're going to try to hang on to your money, your passport, and that set of instructions your mother typed up for you about what to do every minute of your trip, right?

Yeah—all but that last one. Right. But just in case the worst happens, here are some strategies for dealing with all the things— well, most of the things—you could possibly manage to lose while traveling.

Photocopy Everything

This is a general rule which can save you a lot of headaches if you lose any of your important documents: Make photocopies of everything—your passport, airline tickets, confirmation numbers for all reservations, other forms of I.D., insurance cards and information, medical prescriptions, etc. Carry one set of the photocopies in your bag, but not the same bag in which you're carrying the actual documents. Then make your companion carry another set in his or her bag. And finally, leave one set with someone at home who could fax them to you if both you and your travel companion lose everything.

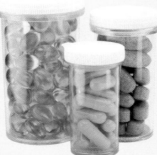

Lost Tickets

The great thing about electronic tickets is that there's no paper ticket to lose. All you really need is your photo I.D., and the airline can pull up your reservation. However, it helps to have your confirmation number when you're checking in, and if you need to change your reservation, your confirmation number will be essential. The problem with paper tickets—and a great reason to avoid them if you can—is that if you lose them, airlines are not obligated to replace them or honor your reservation. (Most airlines will still agree to replace them at the airport if you can show proper identification.) If you're going abroad, the best advice is to treat your tickets like cash. Keep them in a safe place with your other valuables and be mindful of their whereabouts at all times.

Lost Medicine

Always travel with a photocopy of your prescriptions, as well as a letter from your doctor authorizing you to have the copies. If you've got both of these documents, you shouldn't have trouble refilling the prescription in a local pharmacy. Keep medicines in their original vials—in some countries, carrying loose pills can create problems and you could be accused of carrying illegal drugs.

Remember: Important documents should always be packed in your carry-on bag, along with medications and a change of clothes, just in case your luggage is lost or delayed.

Lost Wallets and I.D.

This is basically a nightmare scenario since you can't catch a plane home without a photo I.D., so try to avoid it at all costs. But if you do lose your wallet and I.D., you'll have to do one or more of the following:
1. Contact the authorities in your home state and ask them how long it will take to get a replacement driver's license.
2. Phone a family member or friend and have some money wired to you at a local bank.
3. Phone your credit card company to report the loss, then ask them to overnight a replacement card to you.

Lost Passport

The moment you realize your passport has been lost or stolen, report it to the local police. Then get a copy of the police report—or at least as many details as you can—and a letter from the police confirming the loss of your passport. Take all this info to the local American Consulate or Embassy in the country you're visiting, and apply for a new passport. (For a list of consulates and embassies, go to www.realuguides.com.) A photocopy of your original passport will greatly speed things up.

Lost Luggage

Most lost luggage is reunited with its owners within 48 hours, by fairly straightforward means. Right next to the baggage claim area at most airports, there's a desk marked "Lost Luggage" or something similar. Go there and they may be able to locate your bag right away. If not, leave your local phone number. The airline will call you to let you know the status of your bag, sometimes even phoning in the middle of the night! Most airlines will deliver the bag to you if you ask—you shouldn't have to spend your vacation hiking back to the airport to get it.

However, sometimes bags get lost and never come back, and this is almost always for a very simple reason: They weren't properly identified. You can prevent this by putting a luggage tag on both the handle or strap of the bag *and* inside the bag. Handles and straps are notorious for coming off, but bags labeled clearly on the inside can still be identified.

STREET SMARTS: AVOIDING DANGEROUS SITUATIONS

The best way to avoid real emergency situations is to keep yourself out of trouble in the first place.

Of course, this doesn't mean huddling in your hotel room with the shades drawn and a wet towel around the door frame, because frankly, you could slip in the bathtub and break your leg and no one would find you for days.

No, you're better off on the streets, where at least someone will notice if you trip and break your leg. Here are some tips for staying out of trouble:

■ The concept of safety in numbers works on two levels. First, it's always a good idea to have a companion with you if you're walking around an unfamiliar city. Second, areas that are densely populated with a lot of foot traffic are generally a lot safer than deserted streets and neighborhoods. Stick together and stick to the main roads.

■ Trust your instincts: If you have a feeling that a certain area isn't safe, you're probably right. Turn around and head for safety.

■ Be particularly wary when using ATM's. Cancel your transaction and get out of there if anything makes you uncomfortable.

■ Look both ways—and not just when crossing the street. Pay attention to your surroundings and you'll be better able to anticipate when you're walking into trouble.

■ Although there are exceptions, many U.S. cities are arranged with rougher, more industrial neighborhoods on the south side of the city, and less dangerous neighborhoods on the north. If you get lost in a neighborhood you think is a bit dodgy and all else fails, go north.

TELL ME
WHERE IT HURTS

The first thing you should do if you get sick while you're traveling is call your doctor at home. He or she may be able to diagnose you over the phone, and advise you about what to do next.

However, if you get in a real bind and have to go to a local doctor or hospital, it will help to know what kind of insurance coverage you have. Here are some tips:

- Before you leave, call your insurance company and find out what kind of coverage you have when you're away from your home state. The answer will vary widely, but good plans will at least offer some emergency coverage for other states, although they may pay nothing for medical coverage overseas.

- If you're not insured, or if your insurance doesn't offer you any coverage outside of your home state, you may want to take out additional traveler's insurance.

- One of the best travel insurance programs is offered by International SOS, one of the largest travel assistance companies in the world. For $55, travelers can purchase an ISOS membership for a trip lasting up to fourteen days. This offers telephone access to doctors and nurses who are on call 24 hours, and who can refer you to local doctors. International SOS also provides a host of other rescue and assistance services. For more info, check out www.internationalsos.com.

- Another travel insurance company that provides a useful service is MedJetAssistance. If you get sick or injured overseas, the MedJet policy will provide a medically equipped jet to fly to your location and fly you back to the medical facility and doctor of your choice. Check out more info at www.MedJetAssistance.com.

- In addition to travel medical insurance, you should also always carry a portable first aid kit with basic medical supplies like bandages, gauze, headache pills, motion sickness pills, and a list of emergency phone numbers for the cities and countries you plan to visit. You'll know why this is a good idea if you ever have to spend an hour and a half looking for a drug store in Toledo when you've got a paper cut.

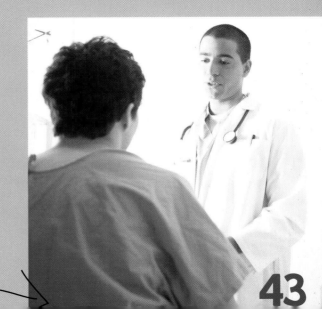

sick as a dog →

43

TRAVELING

ABROAD

If you've done a little traveling in your own country, you've already learned a lot of the skills you'll need in order to travel abroad. However, "crossing the pond" requires a few extra skills and a little bit more planning.

Our best advice about traveling overseas is: Read this chapter first, then buy at least one other guide book about the specific country or countries you're visiting. You don't want to fly all the way to Cancun and forget to see the Mayan ruins, right? Or catch a boat to the Caribbean and fail to notice that there's some awesome snorkeling right under your nose! The trick to having a great trip abroad is to plan ahead, so you know what to expect. But each country is different, so you'll want to do some research about the specific travel requirements, weather, sites, attractions, restaurants, and so forth for the hot spot you're planning to visit.

Meanwhile, we've got a ton of great tips for navigating foreign train stations, dealing with customs, packing like a pro, getting a passport, phoning home from abroad, and more. So get ready for a crash course on crashing the gates of foreign cities, countries, and continents.

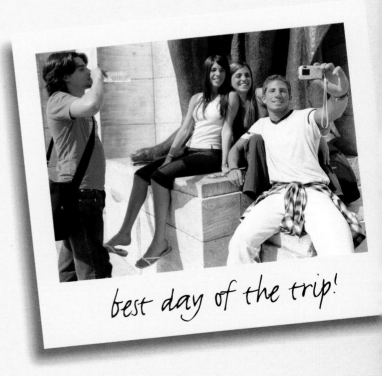

best day of the trip!

SMILE AND SAY CHEESE:
PASSPORTS AND VISAS

PASSORTS

Admit it: You've wanted one of those little blue books with your picture inside and the gold seal on the cover for, like, well, ever. Right? Or maybe you already have a passport, but you've never used it, and the photograph depicts you in the 4th grade, wearing braces and a scab from where you got kicked during a game of dodge ball, and besides, the passport has now expired. Either way, if you're leaving the country, other than to go to Mexico or Canada, you'll need a passport. (For Mexico, you'll need a birth certificate and another form of I.D., so you might as well get a pass-port if you're heading south of the border.) If you're traveling to certain countries, you'll need both a passport (issued by your country) and a visa (issued by the country to which you're traveling).

Getting passports isn't difficult for American citizens. However, it does take time to process them. And if you need it in a hurry, you'll have to pay more for rush service, which is called expedited service. Read on!

■ You can get passport applications online directly from the U.S. Department of State at travel.state.gov/passport. Or you can use a commercial passport service, which will charge a fee but can help expedite it.

■ You have to apply for your first passport in person. This usually means going to a local post office or courthouse. If you're under 18, you may need a parent to accompany you—check the web site. Renewals can be handled by mail.

■ To get a passport, you'll need a certified birth certificate or other proof of U.S. citizenship, and a photo I.D. or other proof of identity. You'll also need two identical passport photos, which you can usually have taken at a copy shop and sometimes at the passport office itself. Check the guidelines on the application for photo size requirements. If you follow the rules and regs carefully, you can take the passport photo yourself with a digital camera. No more deer-in-the-headlights photos—yes!

■ A non-expedited passport is supposed to take 6 weeks, but can take a couple of months to be delivered, so start early.

■ If you need a passport in a hurry, you'll have to expedite it. Basically, you'll have to pay an extra fee in order to have your application rushed through. The U.S. Department of State offers expedited passports, but it still takes 2 weeks.

■ The fastest way these days is to use a commercial passport service, such as www.travisa.com. You'll pay a fee, but can probably get your passport as fast as the next day if you need to.

VISAS

Although a valid American passport will get you past the border of many countries, some countries require both your American passport and a visa, issued by the country itself. The visa can be either a stamp affixed to your passport, or a separate document, but either way it usually means that you have to FedEx your passport to the foreign country's embassy as part of your application. (Don't send your passport in the mail— too risky.) In other words, you've got to get your passport *before* you can get your visa—so plan ahead.

For a list of countries that require visas, visit travel.state.gov/visa/americans.

To get a visa, apply through the foreign country's embassy in the U.S. and pay the fee. Just like passports, visas take a while, but can be expedited for an additional fee. Each country has different requirements for issuing a visa, but you'll often have to provide a printed itinerary from an airline showing when you're entering and leaving the country.

PACKING LIKE A PRO

There are two kinds of airline luggage: carry-on and *lost*. The U.S. Department of Transportation reports that airlines lose or mishandle 7,000 bags a day. So the best thing you can do when packing is to limit your luggage to one carry-on bag.

The next best advice on packing is this: Before you leave, pack everything you want to take with you. Now get rid of half of it. Seriously, packing is part art form, part science, and how well you pack can have a major impact on your travel experience. If you're backpacking around Europe, lugging an 80-pound bag with two cameras and five pairs of shoes, you're going to look back on Paris as a miserable experience.

Here are some general tips. Check out the chart for guidelines for packing for 1-, 2-, and 4-week trips.

■ Always take a sweater and a bathing suit, no matter what climate or time of year. You never know.

■ For a long trip, take along old clothes—especially T-shirts—that you were ready to throw out. Wear them during the first half of the trip and then throw them away! Now you've got room in your bag for that silver candelabra you bought in Spain, or that new Euro-style hoodie you snatched up on sale in Amsterdam.

■ Always pack a camera, travel umbrella, first-aid kit (including antacids and diarrhea medication), and some waterless hand cleaner.

big mistake!

> **The best thing you can do is limit your luggage to one carry-on bag.**

48

1 WEEK

2 pairs jeans or pants
2 T-shirts
1 nice outfit
7 pairs socks
7 pairs underwear
PJ's
1 sweater
1 bathing suit
1 pair comfy walking shoes
1 pair nicer shoes

2 WEEKS

2 pairs jeans or pants
4 T-shirts
2 nice outfits
(you'll get sick of those
T-shirts, trust us)
7 pairs socks—
(wash them out or
wear them twice)
14 pairs underwear
PJ's
1 sweater
1 bathing suit
1 pair comfy walking shoes
1 pair nicer shoes

4 WEEKS

Same as 2 weeks,
but add:
2 more shirts or tops
1 skirt for women or
1 pair of pants for men

DON'T FORGET TO PACK...

- Passport and other I.D.
- Air and train tickets
- Debit and/or credit cards
- Emergency cash/foreign currency
- Photocopies of all important documents (including credit cards, prescriptions, tickets, I.D.'s)

- List of emergency contact info (including embassies abroad and key phone numbers at home—doctors, family members, etc.)
- Health insurance card and info
- Prepaid phone card
- Medications

ANYTHING TO DECLARE? CUSTOMS 101

When your plane lands in a foreign country, you'll have to go through the customs/immigration process before you can leave the airport. Be prepared to wait in (sometimes) long lines, to show identification, and to fill out country-specific forms that ask the purpose of your visit, where you are staying, and how long you will stay. Occasionally, customs officers will inspect your luggage and possessions, although most of the time they simply wave Americans on through.

On your return home, you'll pass through U.S. Customs—the agency responsible for controlling and monitoring the goods that come in and out of the United States. Basically, you're allowed to bring goods purchased abroad back into the country up to a certain dollar amount. If your purchases exceed that limit, you have to declare them to customs upon returning to America, and you'll have to pay a fee (called a "duty") for bringing them into the country. To find out the dollar limits for what you can bring back into the country, go to www.realuguides.com.

One loophole: You can mail things to yourself without paying the duty on them, and you can mail gifts to friends, up to a certain dollar limit.

Customs also regulates certain things that can't be brought into the country, including a lot of food and beverages. You'll find answers to questions about what you can and can't import on the web site listed above.

Another general warning about customs: Almost every major international airport in the Western world uses sniffing dogs to check for illegal substances in carry-on and checked baggage. Don't kid yourself about the seriousness of transporting illegal substances across borders—nor about the likelihood that you'll get caught.

don't try anything funny around him

IMMUNIZATIONS AND TRAVEL

First, some good news: Many countries do not require American travelers to get immunizations. More good news: Many so-called "shots" are actually orally ingested vaccinations. Now the bad news: Many countries do require vaccinations, and yeah, some of them are going to be a sharp stick in the arm. So before you travel, grit your teeth and go to the Centers for Disease Control web site (www.cdc.gov/travel), which maintains a current list of anti-malarial and inoculation requirements, as well as health advisories for specific countries and regions. Once you know which immunizations you'll need, call your doctor to find out the details. Some immunizations require a series of shots several weeks apart, so you may have to start early. If you're going to a country where malaria is present, you'll need to start taking the medicine at least two weeks in advance.

Once you know which immunizations you'll need, call your doctor or health department to find out the details. Keep the immunization card with your passport, and protect it as if it's solid gold. If you lose it and can't prove that you've had the proper shots, you could be denied entry to the country you're visiting, or worse—subjected to immunization at the border by whatever people and equipment they have on hand!

DON'T DRINK THE WATER

Some countries have excellent water treatment plants. Others, less so. Others, not at all. Since you aren't going to hit the shores of a foreign country without reading at least one other travel book about that particular country—remember, you promised!—you'll know before you go whether the water is safe to drink. Here are some guidelines:

■ If you have any doubts, don't drink the tap water.

■ Remember that water served in restaurants may not be safe, and non-brand-name bottled waters, or bottled water without labels, may not be purified. Stick to bottled water from a name brand you recognize.

■ Even brushing your teeth with the tap water may not be a great idea.

■ In some countries, it may be cheaper and easier to purchase iodine or water purification tablets. Unfortunately, they also give water a foul taste and are not recommended for long-term use due to potential adverse health affects.

CLOSE TO THE VEST:
HOW TO PROTECT YOUR VALUABLES

One of the inconveniences of being footloose and out on your own is that you have to carry everything valuable with you at all times. And although you may think that the front pocket on your cargo pants is completely invulnerable to theft or loss, you'll have a hard time explaining that to the American Embassy when your passport turns up missing.

The best solution is a money belt—usually a zippered pouch on a strap which can be worn around your waist, inside your clothes. You'll want to keep your passport and other valuables in it at all times. If you're worried about not being able to get to your money when it's time to slip the concierge a couple Euros, put some cash for the next few hours in your pockets, and then keep everything else in the money belt.

One note: If you're tempted to use one of those security pouches that are usually worn around your neck on a string, never wear it outside your clothes. These are only safe when worn inside your clothes, with your shirt tucked into your pants. Otherwise, the pouch can be easily yanked off your neck, or the cord can be cut and the pouch will fall to the ground.

TIPS FOR TIPPING

Yeah, we know. You're on a budget, and the only tip you'd like to give that Italian waiter is, "Keep your hands off my rump roast."

But if you think that being young and being a first-time traveler gives you an excuse to opt out of the whole tipping game, think again. Otherwise, you'll have no one but yourself to blame when everyone treats you like you're...well, young. And, well, a first-time traveler.

The good news is that in many countries, especially in Europe, most of the "service" is "compris" as the French would say—or in other words, the tip has already been added to the check. (This is true at restaurants and hotels). You may want to leave a few coins or a few Euros on the table in addition to paying the check, but it doesn't need to be 15% of the bill. In hotels, it's nice to leave something extra for the chambermaids, although the service charge is supposed to cover their service. Overall, people in many countries don't expect to be tipped as often as Americans do, so you probably don't have to worry about it too much.

But just remember: Even if you're on a budget, giving whatever tip you can afford shows that at least you understand the system, and you want to be treated like an adult. It may actually mean you get better service, too.

CHANGING MONEY

If you've got an ATM card with a Star, Cirrus, or Plus logo on the back, you're ready to join the new revolution in currency exchange: international ATM's. Before international ATM networks sprang up, you had to exchange cash or traveler's checks at a bank or other currency exchange. Either way, you'd usually be charged a fee, and you wouldn't get the best exchange rates. ATM's have changed all that. Now they give the best rates, and they charge lower fees than other currency exchange outlets.

However, it's still a good idea to carry some money in traveler's checks as an emergency back-up, or to exchange a little bit of cash at your local bank before you leave the U.S. That way you can begin to familiarize yourself with the currency, so you know that 10 Euro bill from the 10,000. And you won't have to try to find an ATM at the airport in order to pay for a taxi.

USING CREDIT CARDS ABROAD

Although ATM cards have become the best deal when it comes to changing money, credit cards don't work the same way. A current trend among many credit card companies is to add "transaction fees" for purchases made in foreign countries. Check your credit card policy before you leave to find out whether the only thing you'll have to declare upon returning through customs is your poverty.

EUROPEAN TRAIN TRAVEL 101

Traveling by train is the most economical way to get around Europe. And once you get the hang of a few basics, it's also the easiest and one of the most fun. Here are some tips for surviving train stations throughout Europe.

▪ Ticket sellers in many European countries will speak little or no English. Consequently, you're going to end up using ridiculous sign language in the train station, then buying 4 tickets to a part of Hungary you weren't planning to visit. Avoid this scenario by buying your train tickets in advance, before you leave the States (if you have a carefully planned trip), or by buying a Eurail Pass.

▪ Unlike train station clerks, the personnel at many large European hotels will almost certainly speak English, and can help you with train reservations if you're making decisions on the fly.

▪ Train tickets in Europe are either first or second class. First class seats are slightly larger and softer than second class seats, and first class compartments are generally much less crowded than second class compartments. First and second class compartments are generally marked on the outside of the train—be sure you get into the right compartment.

▪ Once you've got your ticket, all you need to know is what platform your train is leaving from. This will be listed on a big board in the station, which will show the destinations and departure platforms for each train. (It may help to know the word "platform" or "track" in several languages. See our handy lexicon on the opposite page.)

▪ At the entrance to each platform in many countries, you'll see a short electronic machine for validating tickets. You'll also notice that people are running their tickets through it, or having them stamped by an attendant. This is called validating your ticket, and you must do it before getting on the train or you'll pay a (sometimes hefty) penalty.

EURAIL PASSES

A Eurail pass is a prepaid ticket that lets you travel on trains throughout Europe. They generally offer unlimited travel over a set period of time. There are dozens of different Eurail packages, which allow different kinds of travel—some for traveling within single countries, some for traveling between a couple countries, and some for traveling throughout Europe. Some Eurail passes are for 7 or 14 days, others for a month. Most Eurail passes are good for first class seats. However, remember that having a Eurail pass does not guarantee a seat on the train! You may still need to make a seat reservation in advance, or risk either not getting a seat or being kicked out of your seat at a stop in the middle of your journey! For more info on Eurail passes, check out www.eurail.com.

The great thing about getting around Europe is that signs in airports and train stations are clear and well marked.

WHERE'S THE EXIT? KEY WORDS IN FOUR LANGUAGES

	FRENCH	SPANISH	ITALIAN	GERMAN
Ticket	Billet	Billete/ Boleto	Biglietto	Karte
Platform/Track	Quai/Voie	Plataforma	Binario	Bahnsteig
Restaurant	Restaurant	Restaurante	Ristorante	Gaststatte
Restroom (Men, Women)	Toilettes (Hommes, Dames)	Servicio (Caballeros, Damas)	Gabinetto (Uomo, Donna)	Toilette (Herren, Damen)
Exit	Sortie	Salida	Uscita	Ausgang
Departures	Depart	Salidas	Partenze	Abfarht
Arrivals	Arrivee	Llegadas	Arrivi	Ankunft
Forbidden /Prohibited	Interdit	Se prohibe	Vietato	Verboten
English	Anglais	Ingles	Inglese	Englisch

PHONING HOME

Of course everyone goes traveling to get away from home, but that's no reason you shouldn't call your poor mother and tell her how you're doing. Here are some tips:

- The easiest and best way to make calls from a foreign country back to the U.S. is to use a pre-paid calling card in a public telephone.

- Pre-paid calling cards can be purchased before you leave the U.S. It's probably a good idea to buy one in advance, so you'll be able to make calls easily and quickly in an emergency.

- Once you reach your destination, you may find better deals on phone cards. They're often available at the airport, drug stores, and small newsstands.

- Rates vary widely—shop around.

- Phone cards purchased in one foreign country may not work in a neighboring country—you'll have to buy another card. Keep this in mind if you're traveling to multiple destinations.

- Some calling cards require that you dial an access code. Others work without access codes—just slip them into the payphone and dial the country code and telephone number.

- The instructions on foreign cards, and the voice instructions on the phone, will be given in that country's language. If you make enough mistakes while dialing, however, you may be given the instructions in English!

- Never make calls from a hotel unless you're certain the hotel doesn't impose a surcharge—these fees can be quite hefty and most hotels impose surcharges. One option: Send an email to the U.S. with your hotel phone and room number and let your family call you.

- You may have a mobile phone that works overseas, but be wary: Unless you have a special deal with your mobile carrier, you're looking at a cost of sometimes $10 per minute.

- Although not quite the same as a phone call, e-mail is relatively easy to send from Europe due to the preponderance of local Internet cafés. Although rates vary, you can definitely save time by writing one quick e-mail and sending it to everyone you know, just to make them jealous of your cool trip.

The best way to make calls from Europe is a calling card. Mobile phone calls could cost you $10 per minute!

THE LONG, FOREIGN ARM OF THE LAW

You've probably guessed that American citizens don't have special privileges in, say, North Korea. However, what you probably didn't guess is that they don't have special privileges in France, either. Or even England. Or Canada. Get over it!

In other words, whenever you're traveling abroad, you're implicitly agreeing to abide by the laws of the country you're visiting. So you might want to memorize this piece of advice: Be very respectful of laws (and law enforcement officers) while traveling abroad. If you do run into trouble with the law, contact the American Embassy as soon as you can. However, they may not be able to help you, so the best bet is, as always, to stay out of trouble with the Man in the first place.

CONTACTING THE EMBASSY: HOW AND WHY

The most obvious reason for contacting the embassy is if you lose your passport. See Page 41 for more details. Since the last thing you want to do in an emergency is have to look up embassy phone numbers in a foreign telephone directory, it's a good idea to travel with several copies of the embassy telephone number, in different parts of your luggage. If push comes to shove, you can get embassy numbers and locations online, at www.travel.state.gov/visa.

You should also contact the embassy first thing in the case of any civil unrest. It may not necessarily be a good idea to go to the embassy, however, at times of civil unrest, since embassies are often targets. But calling the embassy should give you the necessary information about what the State Department recommends.

ALONE

TOGETHER: TRAVELING WITH FRIENDS

The problem with traveling alone is that you almost always end up wishing you had someone with whom you could share your experiences. Of course, the problem with traveling with your friends is that you almost always end up wishing that for just ten blasted minutes—ten minutes, that's all you ask—you could be alone with your experiences.

The trick, then, is to pick travel partners who are suited to your own personal travel style—whatever that is.

Although a little chafing between friends on a trip is as inevitable as a little chafing between your shoulder and the strap on your backpack, you want to avoid going on long trips with someone who's likely to push you over the edge. So don't start singing "Come Fly With Me" till you've read this chapter on how to get along once you're on the road.

great moments...

VERY CAREFULLY: HOW TO CHOOSE A TRAVEL-MATE

Your best friend and current roommate, who's seen what you're really like in the morning, is going to make one kind of travel companion. Your seems-nice office co-worker who once went to a concert with you and hogged all the nachos that night will probably make another. Here's a checklist of what to look for in an ideal travel companion. See how many of these qualities are true about the person you're thinking of hitting the road with—before you hit the road.

Of course, no travel companion is perfect—you may have a friend who meets some of these criteria but not others, or you may not know whether your friend meets them. Nevertheless, these questions should get you started thinking about the kind of friendship that can survive the stress of being trapped in close proximity under unfamiliar conditions for weeks and weeks and weeks at a time.

	TRUE	FALSE
You've known him/her for a long time and know his/her daily habits very well.	☐	☐
You like doing the same things when you're at home together.	☐	☐
You need about the same amount of sleep as he/she does.	☐	☐
He/she doesn't snore.	☐	☐
When you get lunch together, there's usually no argument about who will pick up the bill—you split it, or if you don't, you alternate paying each time you go out.	☐	☐
He/she has seen you at your worst, and you didn't mind. Your relationship has already survived some tough times.	☐	☐
You are not carrying an unrequited torch for him/her, the same torch you have been carrying since the 2nd grade, and which you've never brought yourself to confess.	☐	☐

HE LOVES ME, HE LOVES ME NOT:
TRAVELING WITH BOYFRIENDS OR GIRLFRIENDS

Of course, the stress that travel can put on a relationship doubles when that relationship is a romantic one. After all, you'll be waking up in a hostel having not showered for three days with the person you most want to impress, not just your dingy best friend who rarely showers anyway. But the basic criteria for judging whether your boy toy is travel companion material aren't too different from the criteria for picking any travel companion: Do you know and get along with his/her daily habits? Can the two of you deal with money together without conflict? Has your relationship already survived stress?

The fact is that taking a long trip with your boyfriend or girlfriend will most likely either bond you together for a long time or split you up faster than you can say "bon voyage." You could risk it and end up with some great memories, or you could leave your love slave at home and write scintillating postcards—which might be better for the relationship, anyway. (And by the way, those scintillating postcards might sound like a pretty good idea once you've checked out the singles scene in Cancun.)

6 ROAD RULES

OR HOW TO TRAVEL WITH FRIENDS AND NOT END UP HATING EACH OTHER

Now that you've picked your ideal traveling companion, everything should go smoothly, right? Well, it depends—are you an ideal traveling companion?

Getting along when you're traveling with someone is all about making compromises and setting boundaries. Here are some tips for getting through the trip with your friendship intact.

1 PLAN AHEAD

Talk about where you want to go before you get on the plane. No one likes having plans sprung on them at the last minute, and compromises are easier to make when you've got some time to prepare for them. Talk about it in advance, and maybe the International Museum of Rope and String won't sound quite so crazy by the time you get there.

2 KEEP IT SMALL

Traveling with one or two friends is tough enough. Traveling in a group can be a royal pain. Unless you're all together on an organized trip, you might be wise to avoid that particular challenge.

3 DIVIDE EXPENSES FAIRLY

The easiest way to do this is to pay for things separately as often as you can. Things like meals, museum admissions, and souvenirs can easily be split and paid for separately. If one of you pays for a large shared expense, like a rental car or a hotel, keep a record of the transaction and settle it as soon as you can. If the group wants to participate in an activity and you can't afford it, don't be afraid to opt out and meet up with them later—a certain amount of independence is good for the group, anyway.

4 MAKE DECISIONS TOGETHER

The single best advice about making decisions with your travel buddy is to compromise until you can both agree. That's usually not a problem if you both want to do the same thing, but if for some reason you want to stay in Prague and your friend wants to go to Paris, you need to agree that splitting up is the best idea. If you both don't agree on that, then one of you needs to make a compromise for the ultimate good of the entire trip. If you can handle leaving Prague (not the worst thing that ever happened), hopefully your friend will acknowledge this concession and give in to something you want to do down the road.

5 TAKE A BREATHER

The best solution to a conflict during your trip may well be to take some time off. Talk to your friend and tell him/her that you're going to spend a day out on your own, and then do it. Take a side trip into the country, spend the day wandering a museum, drown your sorrows at the local pub—anything to get some time on your own. Even if you're not in the midst of a spat, spending some time on your own may be just the thing to put the spice back in your travel relationship—and it's a great way to solve the very simple problem that you want to see the Louvre and your friend wants to see the Louis Vuitton store.

6 DISCUSS MONEY IN ADVANCE

Not the amount you wish you could spend—the amount you can actually spend. This may be slightly awkward, because not everyone you travel with will have the same resources. Nevertheless, having an honest talk before you leave about what you can and can't afford will save you a lot more awkwardness down the road.

Bon voyage and happy trails...

MORE REAL U...

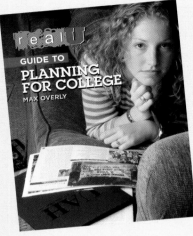

PLANNING FOR COLLEGE

Don't stress about college. Take the anxiety down a notch with this excellent step-by-step guide filled with great tips that increase your chances of getting into your top-choice school. With a timeline for high school freshmen, sophomores, juniors, and seniors—plus great advice about acing the college interview, writing great essays, dealing with the SAT's, and much more. Includes a clear and concise overview of financial aid

YOUR FIRST APARTMENT

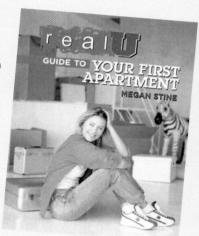

Whether you're leaving home for the first time, heading off to college... or skipping the college thing and sliding straight into a real job and real life, this guide has everything you need to know to move out of the house and start your life for real.

CHECK OUT THESE OTHER REAL U GUIDES!

Bank Accounts and Credit Cards

Living on Your Own

Saving and Investing

Buying Your First Car

Road Safety and Car Care

Your First Job

Identity Theft